WHITE HOUSE INSIDERS

What's It Like to Be the
PRESIDENT'S PET?

BY KATHLEEN CONNORS

Gareth Stevens
PUBLISHING

Please visit our website, www.garethstevens.com. For a free color catalog of all our high-quality books, call toll free 1-800-542-2595 or fax 1-877-542-2596.

Library of Congress Cataloging-in-Publication Data

Connors, Kathleen.
What's it like to be the president's pet? / by Kathleen Connors.
   p. cm. — (White House insiders)
Includes index.
ISBN 978-1-4824-1106-5 (pbk.)
ISBN 978-1-4824-1107-2 (6-pack)
ISBN 978-1-4824-1105-8 (library binding)
1. Presidents' pets — United States — Juvenile literature. 2. Presidents — United States — Biography — Anecdotes — Juvenile literature. 3. Pets — United States — Anecdotes — Juvenile literature. I. Connors, Kathleen. II. Title.
E176.48 C66 2014
973—d23

First Edition

Published in 2015 by
Gareth Stevens Publishing
111 East 14th Street, Suite 349
New York, NY 10003

Copyright © 2015 Gareth Stevens Publishing

Designer: Nick Domiano
Editor: Kristen Rajczak

Photo credits: Cover, p. 1 (Bo & Sunny) Pete Souza/White House via Getty Images; cover, p. 1 (Socks the cat) Diana Walker/Time & Life Pictures/Getty Images; cover, p. 1 (Millie the dog) Carol T. Powers/Time & Life Pictures/Getty Images; pp. 5, 20 Stephen Jaffe/AFP/Getty Images; p. 7 (main) Adam Cuerden/Wikimedia Commons; p. 7 (inset) ZooFari/Wikimedia Commons; p. 9 John F. Kennedy Library/Archive Photos/Getty Images; p. 11 VT Historical Society/AP Photos; p. 13 Cynthia Johnson//Time & Life Pictures/Getty Images; p. 15 Drew Angerer-Pool/Getty Images; p. 17 David Valdez/White House/Time & Life Pictures/Getty Images; p. 19 John Greim/LightRocket via Getty Images.

CPSIA compliance information: Batch #CS15GS: For further information contact Gareth Stevens, New York, New York at 1-800-542-2595.

Contents

Animal House 4

Past Pets 6

From Afar 8

It's a Zoo! 10

Home Sweet Home 12

Work and Play 14

Witnesses to History 16

Frequent Flyers 18

Why Pets? 20

Glossary 22

For More Information 23

Index 24

Words in the glossary appear in **bold** type the first time they are used in the text.

Animal House

President Harry Truman once said, "If you want a friend in Washington, get a dog." While not every US president had a dog while in office, pets have been members of most First Families since George Washington, our first president.

In the past, turkeys, sheep, snakes, and other animals have been beloved White House pets. Recent presidents have favored cats and dogs, like President Bill Clinton's chocolate Labrador retriever, Buddy. They're often just as famous as the president!

The Inside Scoop

Since 1800, the US president has lived in the White House. Hundreds of pets have made their homes there, too!

President Clinton and Buddy became pals in December 1997. Buddy was an instant celebrity with his friendly personality and good looks!

5

Past Pets

Presidents' love for animals dates all the way back to George Washington. At his home in Virginia, Washington had many farm animals. He rode his favorite horse, Nelson, to the British **surrender** at Yorktown, Virginia, during the American Revolution. He was also known to love **hounds**! None of these animals lived at the White House, however, because the White House hadn't been built yet.

Thomas Jefferson's pets lived at 1600 Pennsylvania Avenue, though. He had a mockingbird that would eat food from his mouth!

The Inside Scoop

President Abraham Lincoln loved cats. He's said to have **adopted** kittens he found in an office of the war department!

Dash

Benjamin Harrison was president from 1889 to 1893. While he was in office, several dogs lived at the White House, including one named Dash.

7

From Afar

Foreign leaders sometimes give presidents pets as gifts. Perhaps the most famous of these is the alligator given to President John Quincy Adams. President Jefferson kept two bear cubs he'd been given in cages on the White House lawn until a proper home could be found. President Martin Van Buren received tiger cubs!

The leader of the Soviet Union gave a dog, Pushinka, to President John F. Kennedy's daughter, Caroline. Luckily, Pushinka got along with Caroline's other dog, Charlie.

The Inside Scoop

The first Siamese cat in America is thought to have been a gift to President Rutherford Hayes in 1878. A US **diplomat** in Bangkok, Thailand, sent the cat.

Pushinka was one of the Kennedy family's many pets at the White House!

9

It's a Zoo!

Many of the animal gifts presidents receive, like the herd of elephants given to James Buchanan, don't stay at the White House very long. Other rather strange pets have become part of the First Family, though.

Of his many animals, President Calvin Coolidge's favorite pet might have been Rebecca, a raccoon! He would visit her every day and walk her on a leash. Rebecca wasn't the oddest Coolidge family pet. At different times, they had a goose, a pygmy hippo, and a bobcat!

The Inside Scoop

President Zachary Tyler's horse, Old Whitey, liked to snack on the White House lawn. He wasn't the only pet to do so—Woodrow Wilson let Old Ike, a sheep, trim the lawn, too!

This photograph shows First Lady Grace Coolidge holding Rebecca, the Coolidges' beloved pet raccoon.

11

Home Sweet Home

Living at the White House can be quite comfortable for presidential pets. President Ronald Reagan's dog, Rex, had a special doghouse built for him. It had red velvet curtains and framed pictures of the president and First Lady hung in it!

President Lyndon Johnson was well known for spoiling his dogs, Him and Her. They were allowed to swim in the White House pool and took rides in the president's limo. Him and Her played chase in the Oval Office, too!

The Inside Scoop

Rebecca the raccoon rode in a limo, too! President Coolidge worried she would be lonely while he and his wife were away and sent the car to pick her up.

Like many beloved White House pets, Rex was **pampered**!

13

Work and Play

Presidential pets often have scheduled appearances, much like the president and First Lady do. Rex, the Reagan's dog, was "in charge" of lighting the national Christmas tree in 1985.

Playtime is important, too! President Gerald Ford's dog, Liberty, liked to jump into the fountains on the White House lawn to cool off in the summertime. After it snowed one year while President John F. Kennedy was in office, his daughter's pony, Macaroni, pulled the Kennedy kids around in a sleigh on the South Lawn.

The Inside Scoop

Because they're in the spotlight, when a presidential pet does something wrong, everyone knows about it. Major, one of the dogs owned by President Franklin D. Roosevelt's family, bit someone!

Presidential pets are often watched over by the Secret Service security team and White House staff, just like the rest of the First Family. Here, a staff member walks Bo and Sunny, the Obamas' dogs.

15

Witnesses to History

Presidential pets have special opportunities to see history as it happens. Many have spent time lounging in the Oval Office. President Warren Harding's dog, Laddie Boy, attended **Cabinet** meetings and even had his own chair in the room!

In 1941, President Franklin D. Roosevelt and British Prime Minister Winston Churchill signed the Atlantic Charter aboard the USS *Augusta*. This important document said what the two leaders wanted the world to be like after World War II. Fala, President Roosevelt's Scottish terrier, was there, too!

The Inside Scoop
Fala slept at the foot of President Roosevelt's bed.

President George H. W. Bush and Ranger take a look around the Oval Office together in 1993.

17

Frequent Flyers

Fala was always traveling with President Roosevelt! He went to the president's home in Hyde Park, New York, and more exotic places like Mexico; Quebec, Canada; and even overseas.

Dogs Spot and Barney often flew with President George W. Bush to Camp David, the presidential **retreat** in Maryland. Bo, the Obama family's dog, flew in an Osprey helicopter to a vacation spot in Martha's Vineyard, Massachusetts, in 2013. When traveling greater distances, presidents' dogs fly aboard Air Force One with the president!

The Inside Scoop

Air Force One is any plane the president is flying in, though it most often means one of the special Boeing 747-200B planes made just for the president's use.

Today, Fala remains at President Franklin Roosevelt's side. A statue of him sits next to the president on the Franklin Delano Roosevelt Memorial in Washington, DC.

WHO) SEEK TO ESTABLISH
OF GOVERNMENT BASED ON
GIMENTATION OF ALL HUMAN
Y A HANDFUL OF INDIVIDUAL
... CALL THIS A NEW ORDER.
T NEW AND IT IS NOT ORDER.

Why Pets?

Presidential pets are often more than just companions to the First Family. They're a **political** tool. While campaigning for the presidency, Herbert Hoover adopted a dog named King Tut to soften his image. Some **critics** of President George W. Bush said he used his cute Scottish terrier, Barney, to shift attention away from military problems.

Still, pets have been said to ease the president's **stress** and don't judge the president's actions. Sometimes, nothing's better than the friendship of a pet!

Clinton Family with Buddy

The Inside Scoop

Presidential pets often get letters! As First Lady, Hillary Clinton collected some of the letters sent to the Clintons' cat, Socks, and dog, Buddy, into a book.

More About Presidents' Pets

- President John Quincy Adams's wife had pet silkworms.

- President Benjamin Harrison gave his grandchildren a pet goat. One day, the goat was pulling them around in a cart and ran right out the White House gates.

- Fala wasn't the only dog present at the signing of the Atlantic Charter. Winston Churchill's poodle, Rufus, also attended the historic meeting.

- Caroline Kennedy's dog Pushinka was the daughter of Strelka, one of the dogs the Russians sent into space.

- President George H. W. Bush's dog, Millie, had a puppy named Spot while she lived in the White House. Spot moved back to the White House with his owner, the second President Bush!

Glossary

adopt: to make part of a family

Cabinet: the president's closest advisers

critic: a person who finds fault or gives judgment

diplomat: a person who works with other nations

hound: a kind of dog historically used for hunting

pamper: to treat with a lot of care and attention

political: having to do with politics, or the business of the government

retreat: a private place

stress: a state of concern, worry, or feeling nervous

surrender: to give up power to another

For More Information

BOOKS

Barnes, Peter W., and Cheryl Shaw Barnes. *President Adams' Alligator and Other White House Pets*. Washington, DC: Regnery Publishing, 2013.

Moberg, Julia. *Presidential Pets: The Weird, Wacky, Little, Big, Scary, Strange Animals That Have Lived in the White House*. Watertown, MA: Charlesbridge Publishing, 2012.

WEBSITES

Presidential Pet Museum

presidentialpetmuseum.com/
Check out photographs and read lots of information from the Presidential Pet Museum's website.

Presidential Pets

www.whitehouse.gov/photos-and-video/photogallery/presidential-pets
See pictures of past presidents with their pets.

Index

alligator 8

Barney 18, 20

bear cubs 8

Bo 15, 18

bobcat 10

Buddy 4, 5, 20

cats 4, 6, 8, 20

dogs 4, 6, 7, 8,
    12, 14, 15, 16,
    18, 20, 21

elephants 10

Fala 16, 18, 19

goat 21

goose 10

horses 6, 10, 14

mockingbird 6

Pushinka 8, 9, 21

pygmy hippo 10

raccoon 10, 11, 12

Rebecca 10, 11, 12

Rex 12, 13, 14

sheep 4, 10

snakes 4

Socks 20

Sunny 15

tiger cubs 8

turkeys 4